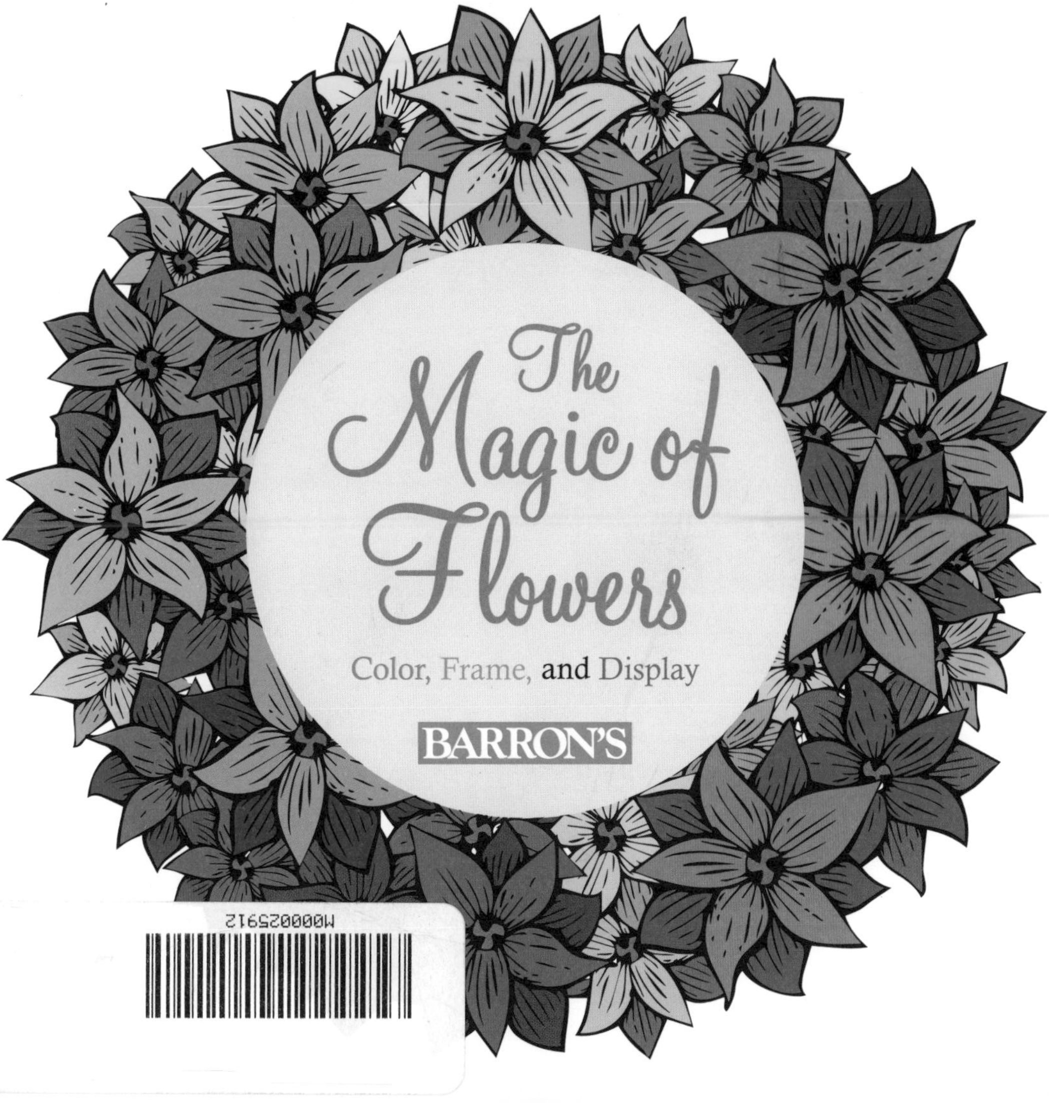

The Magic of Flowers

Color, Frame, and Display

BARRON'S

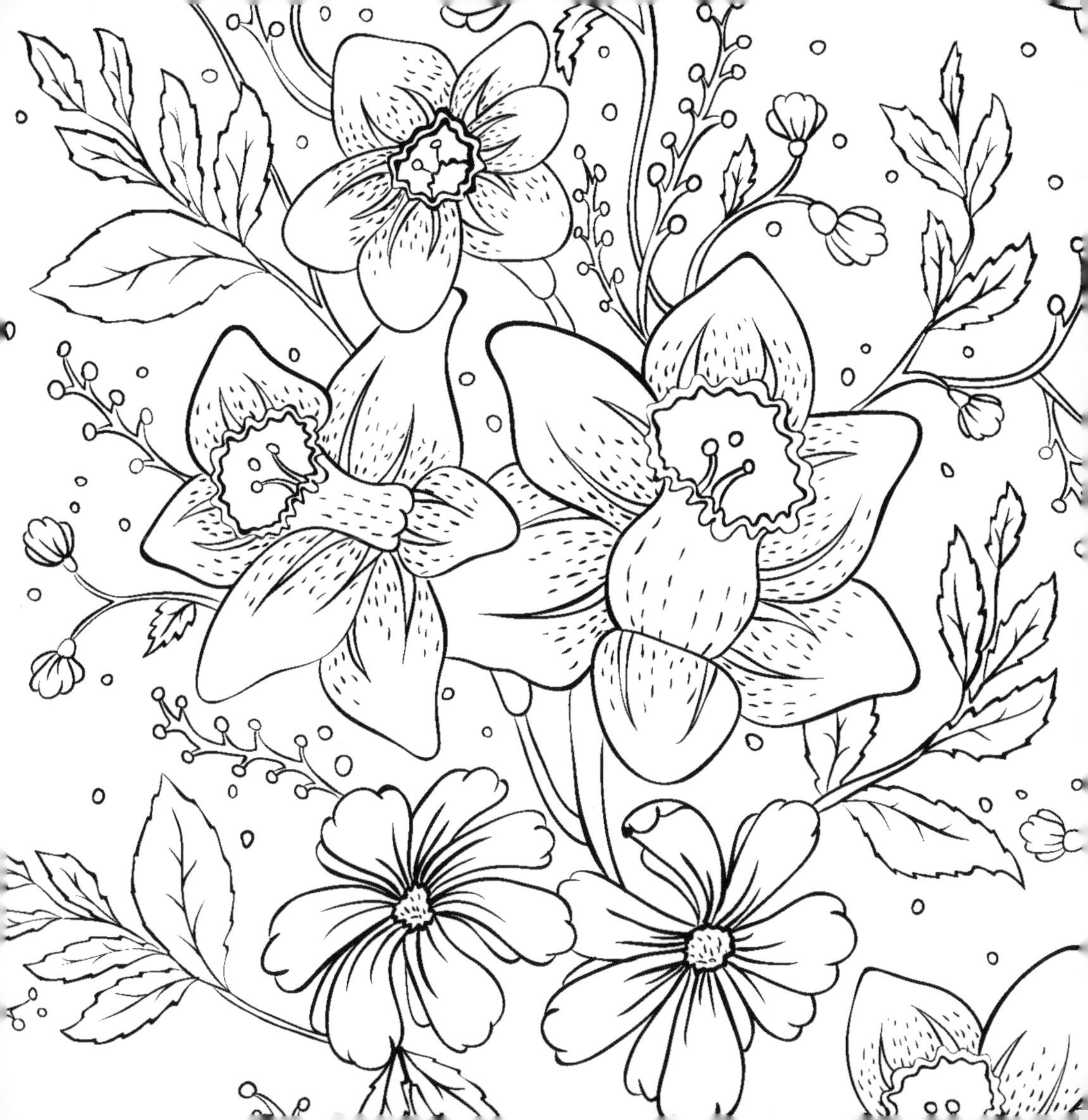

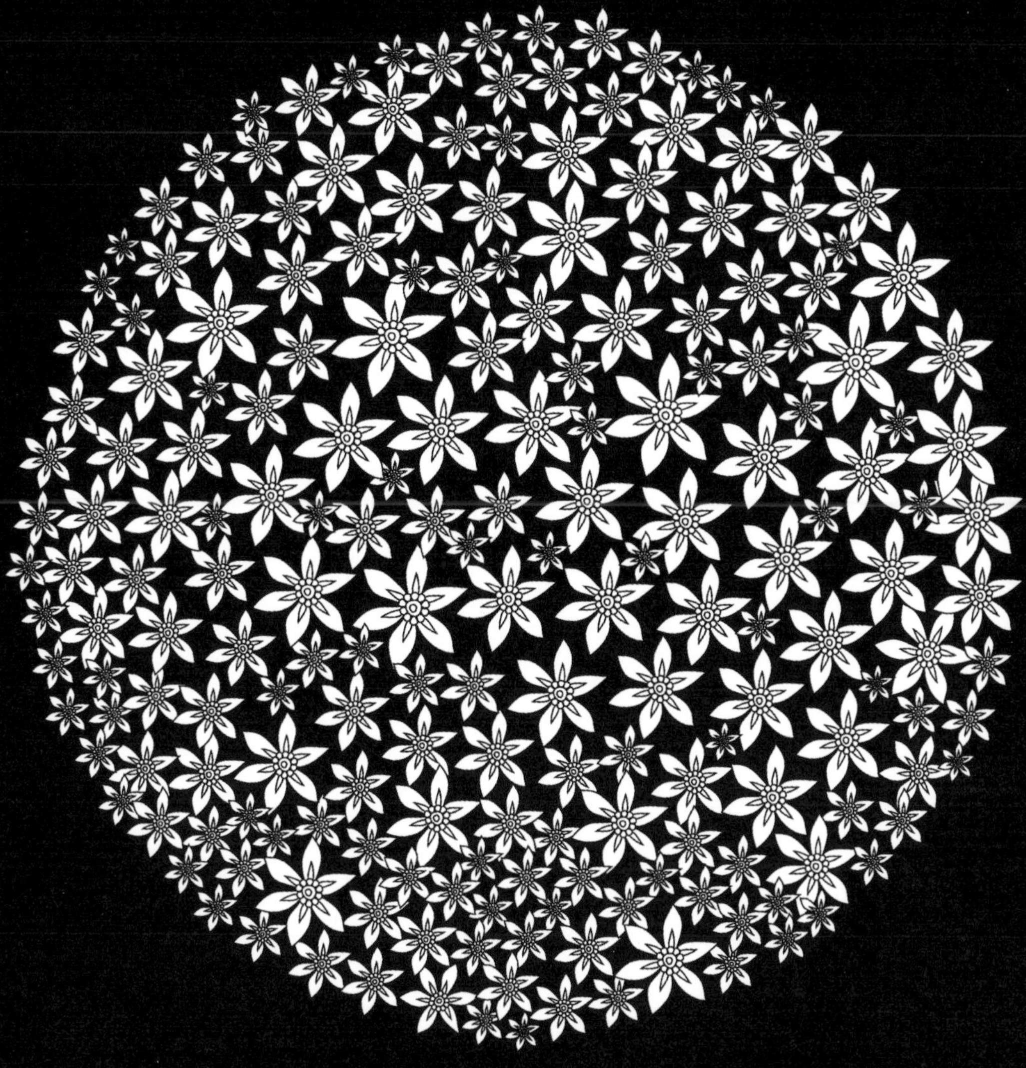

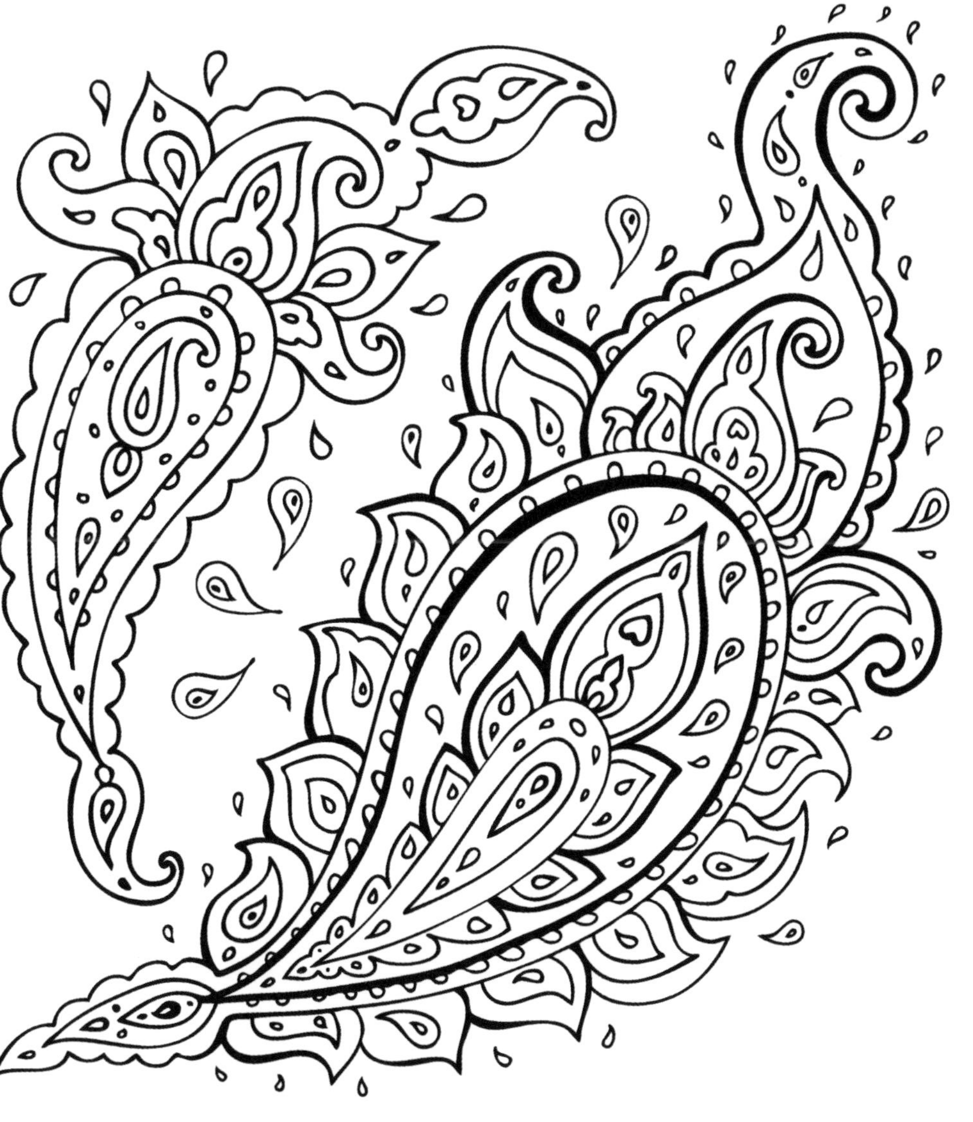

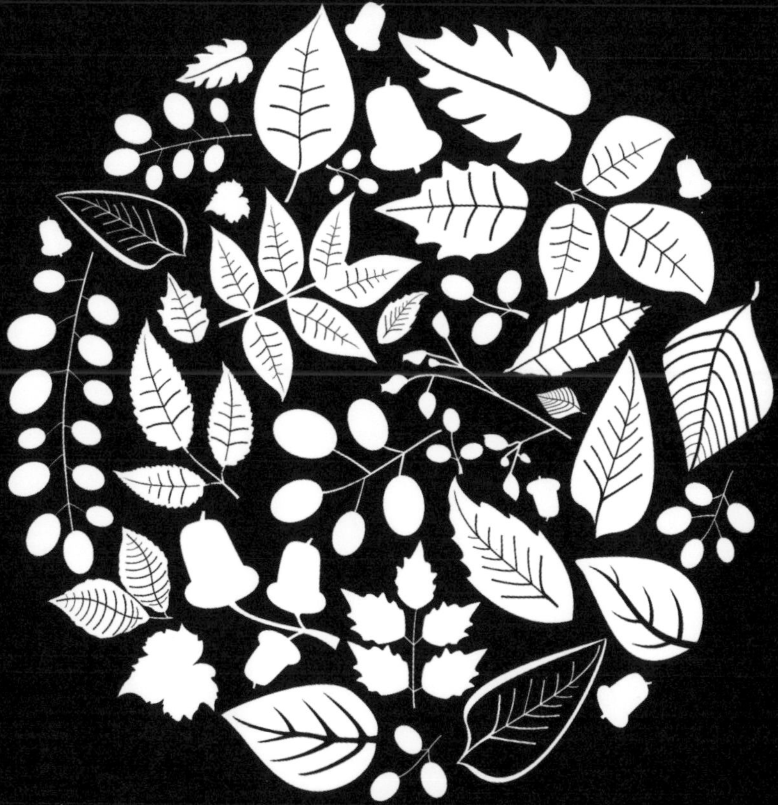

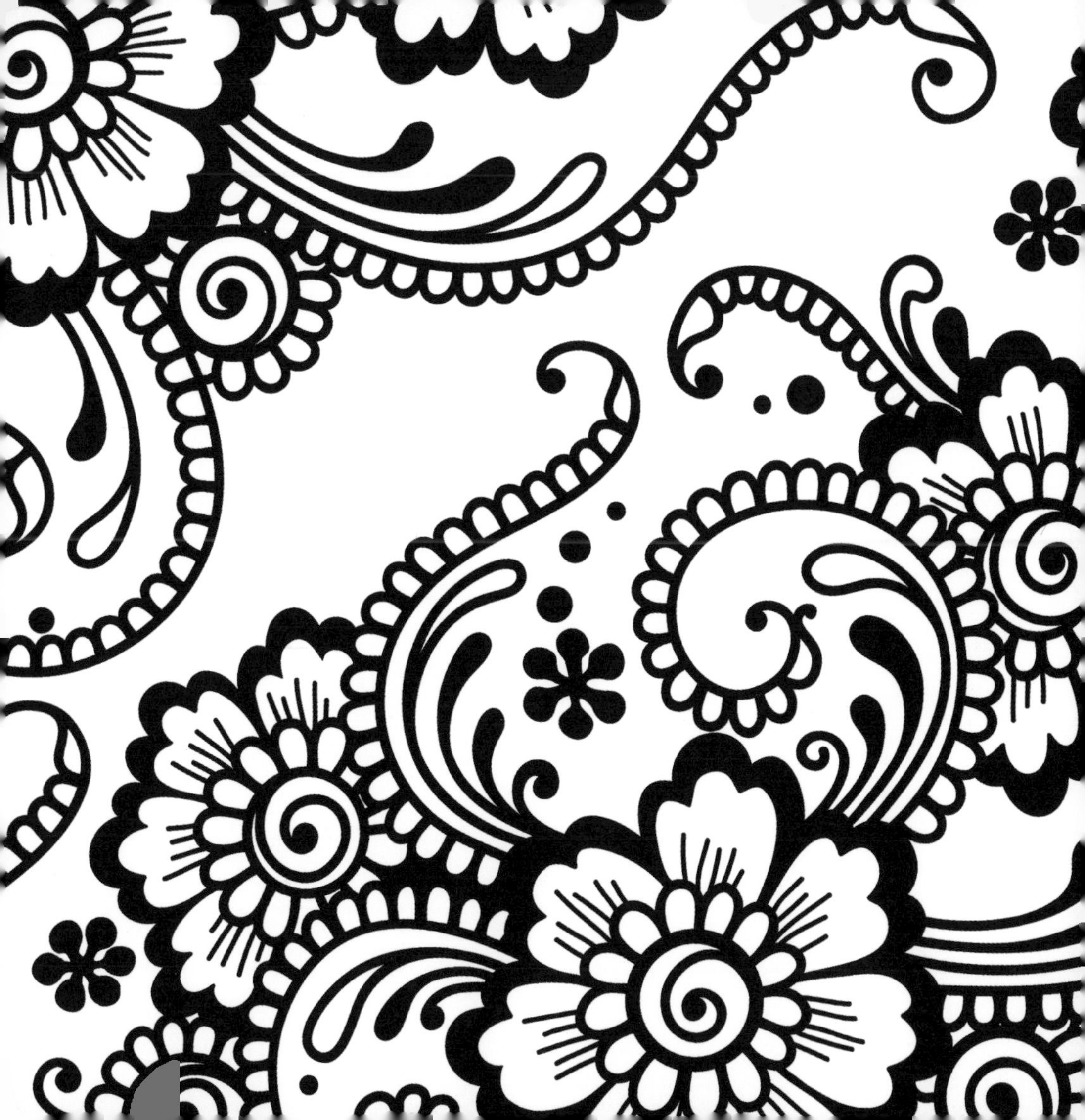

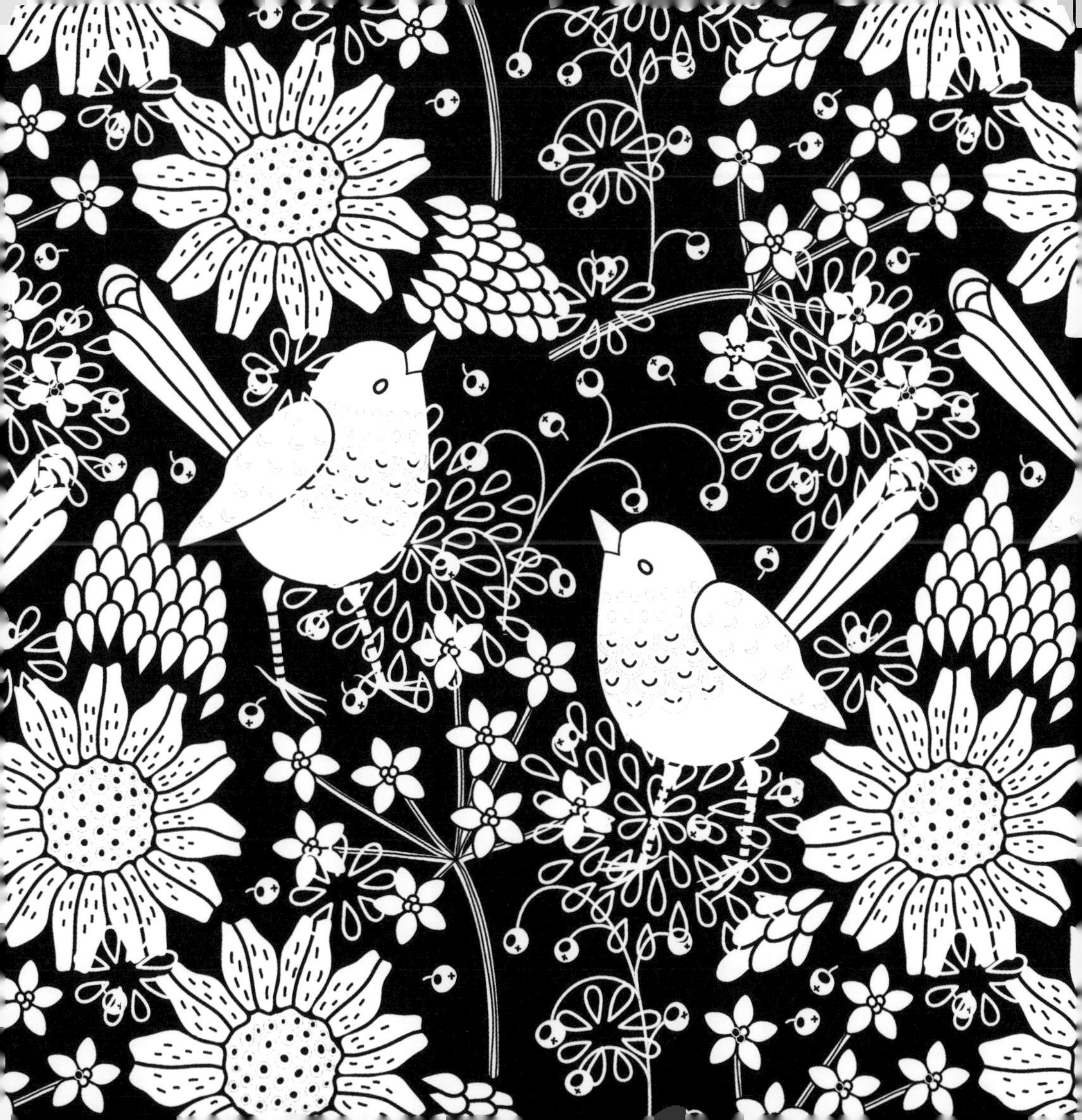

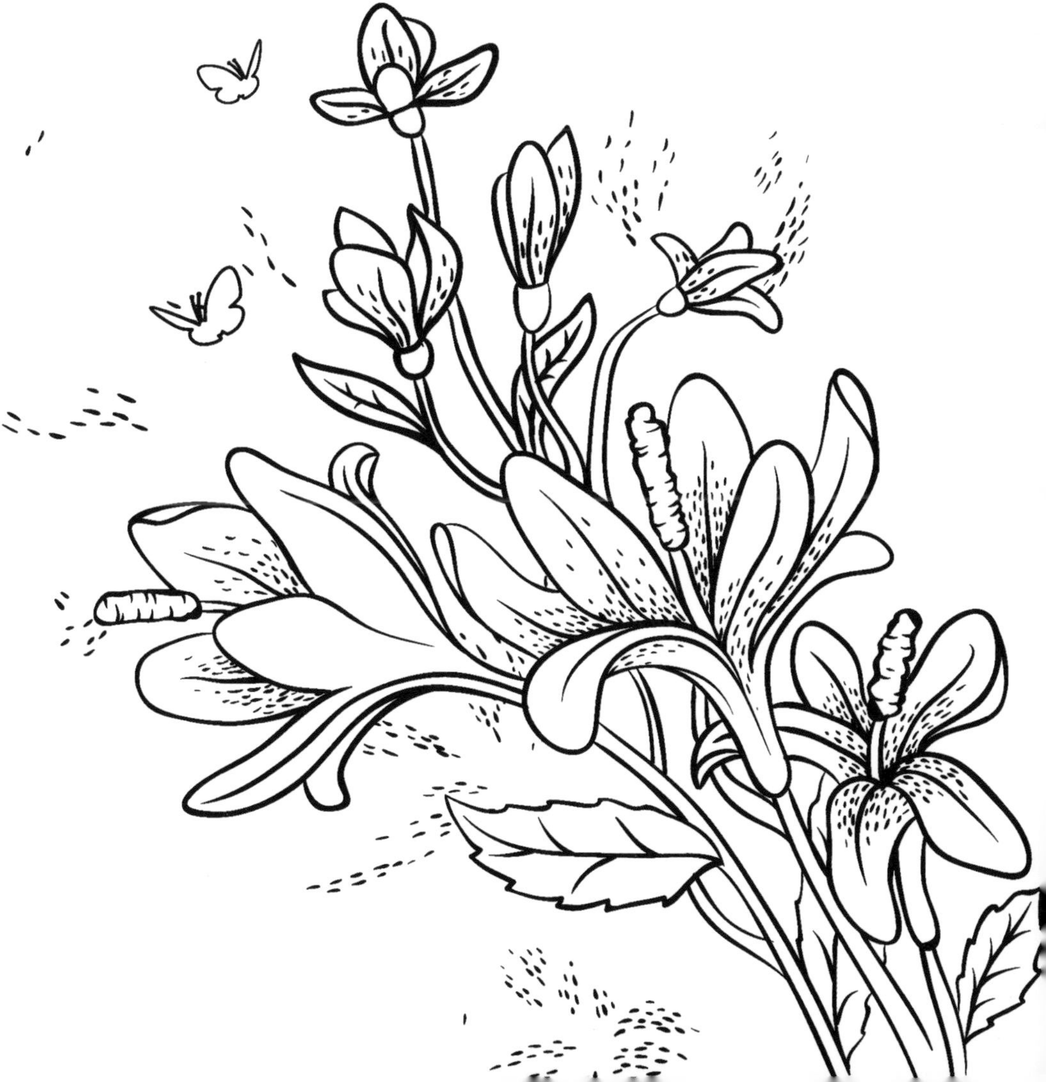

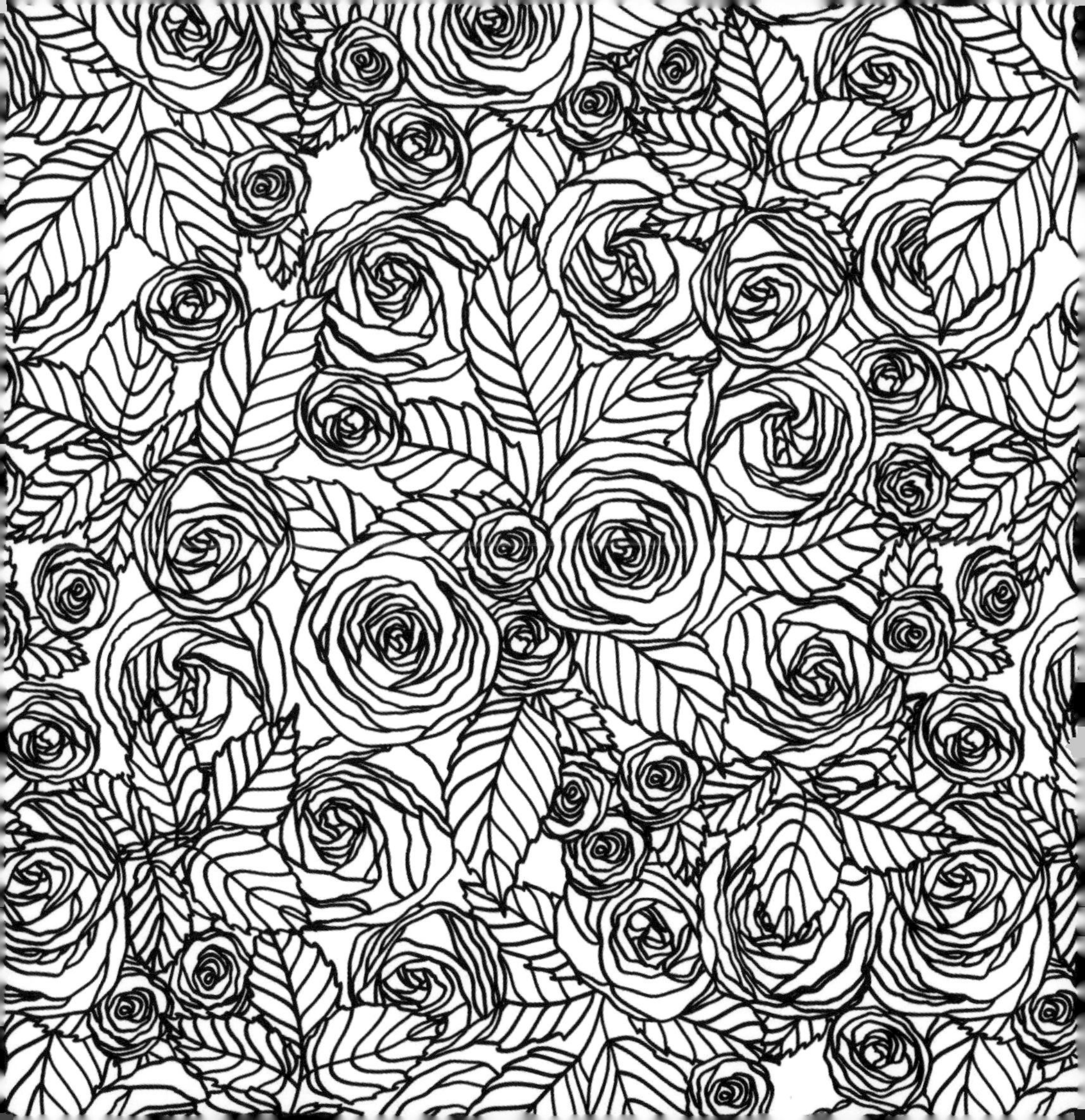

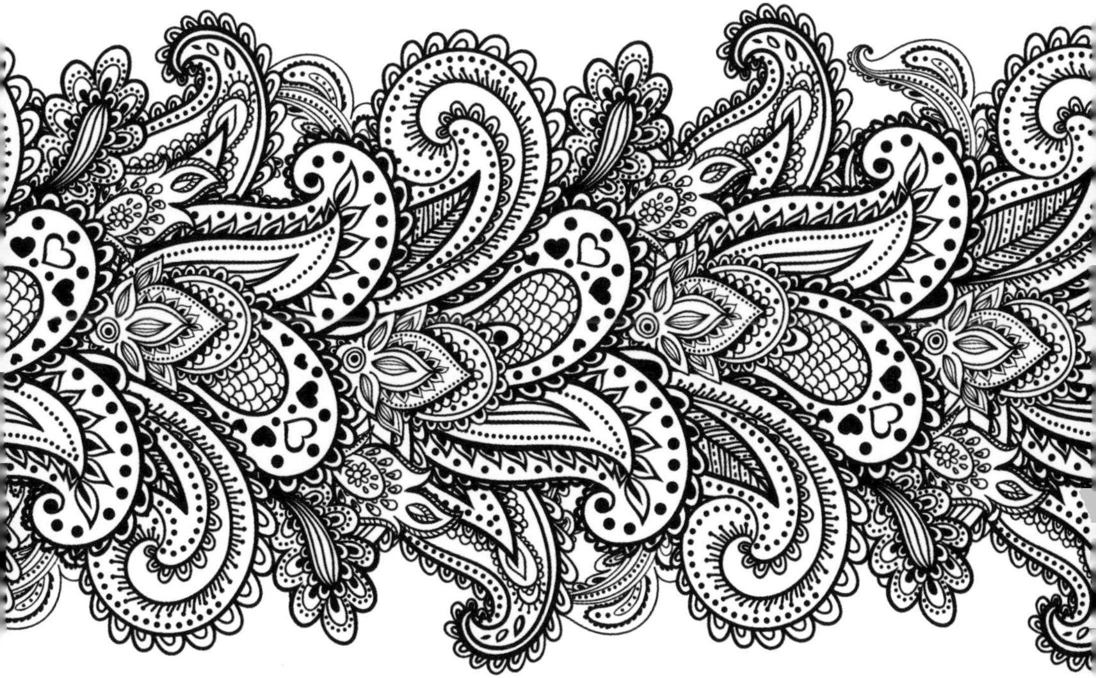

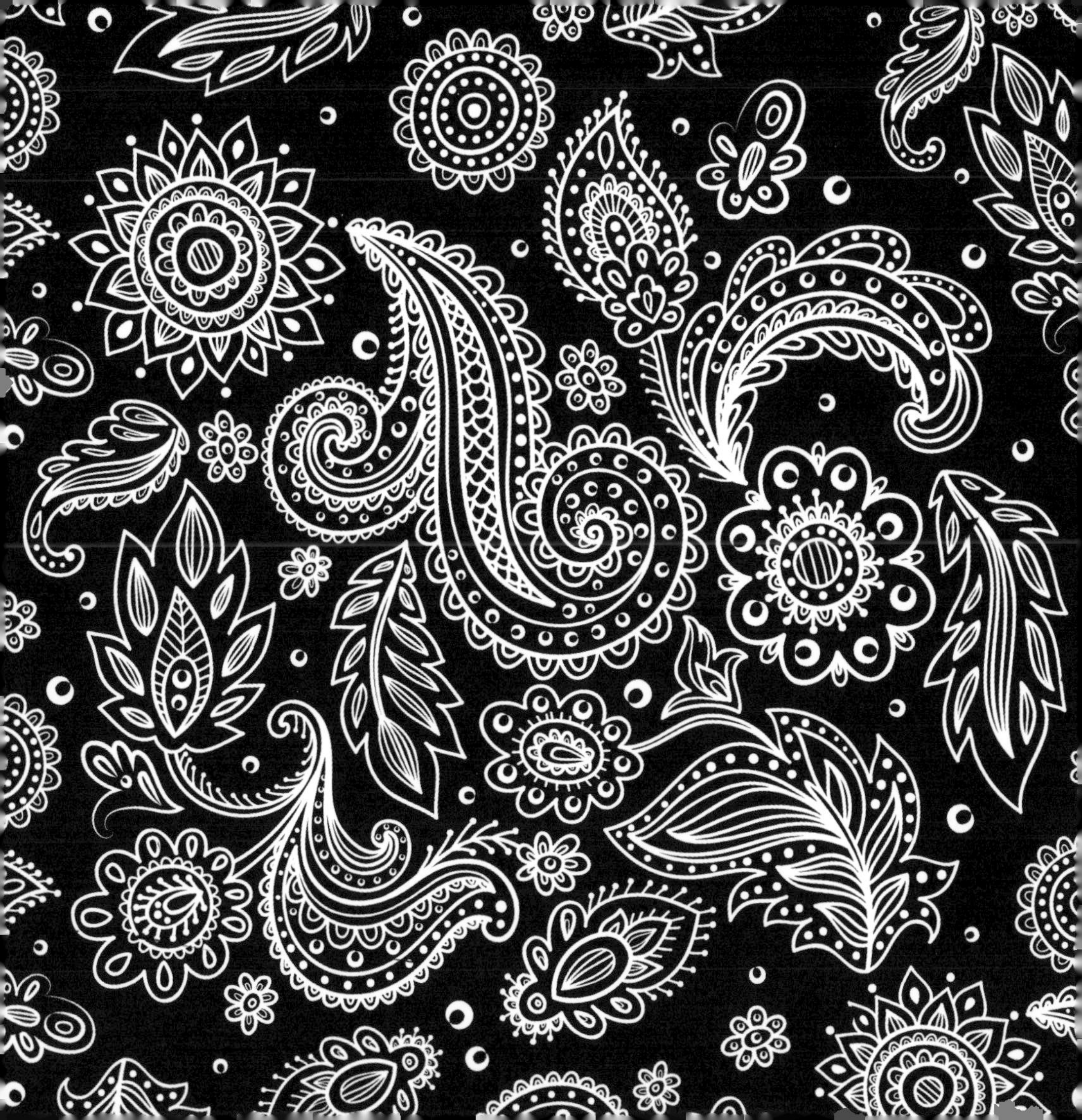

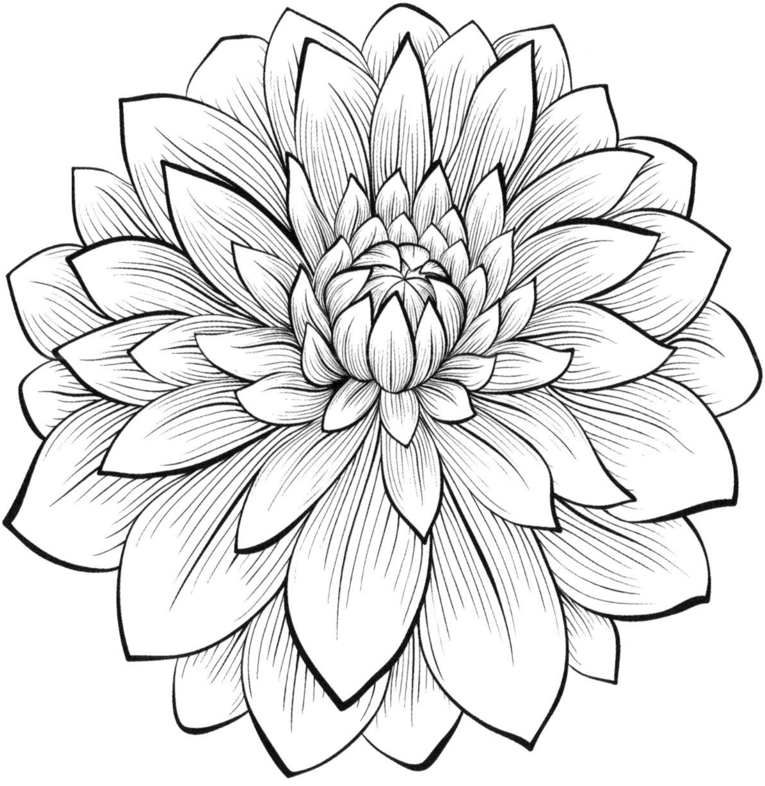

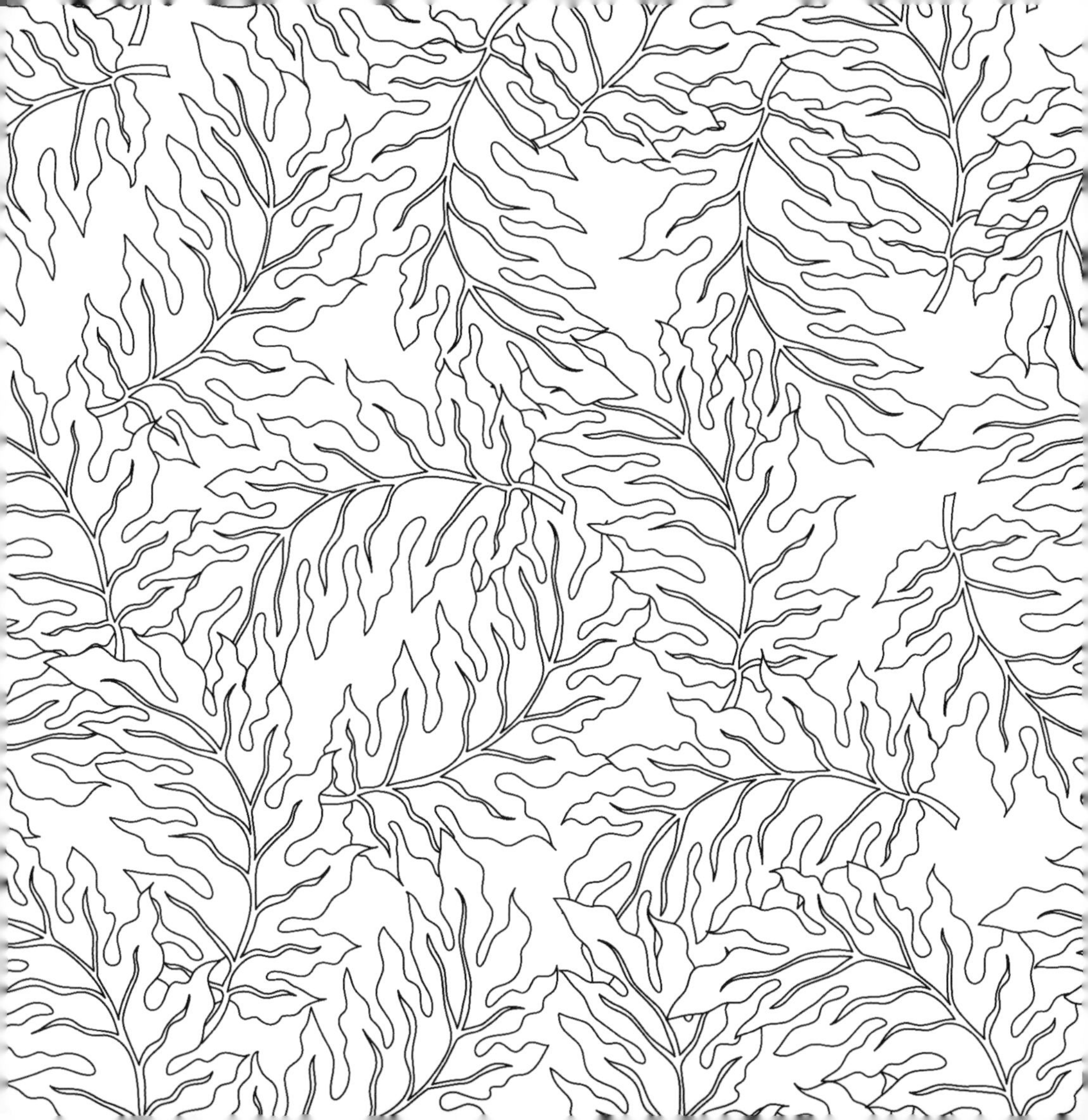

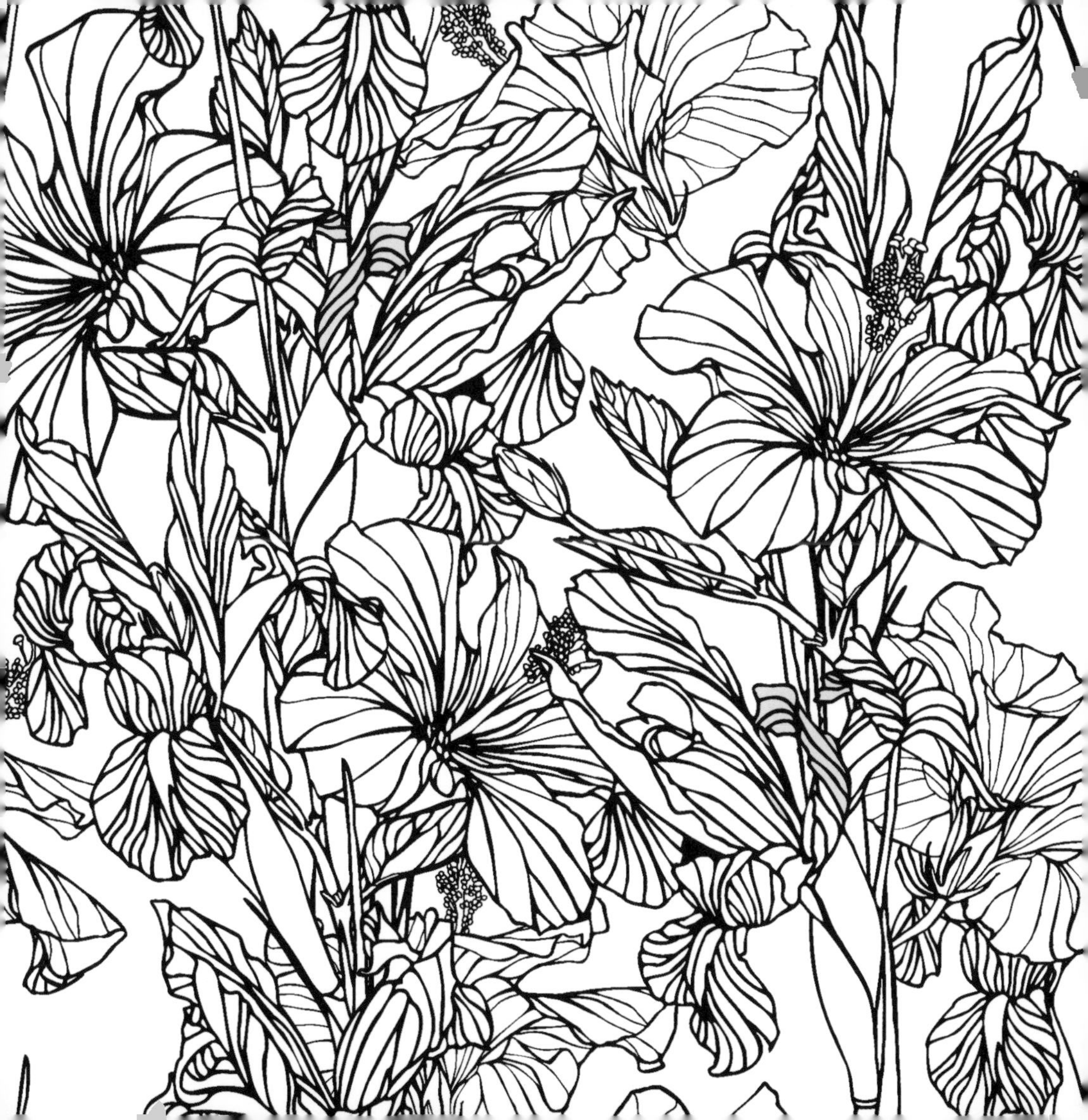

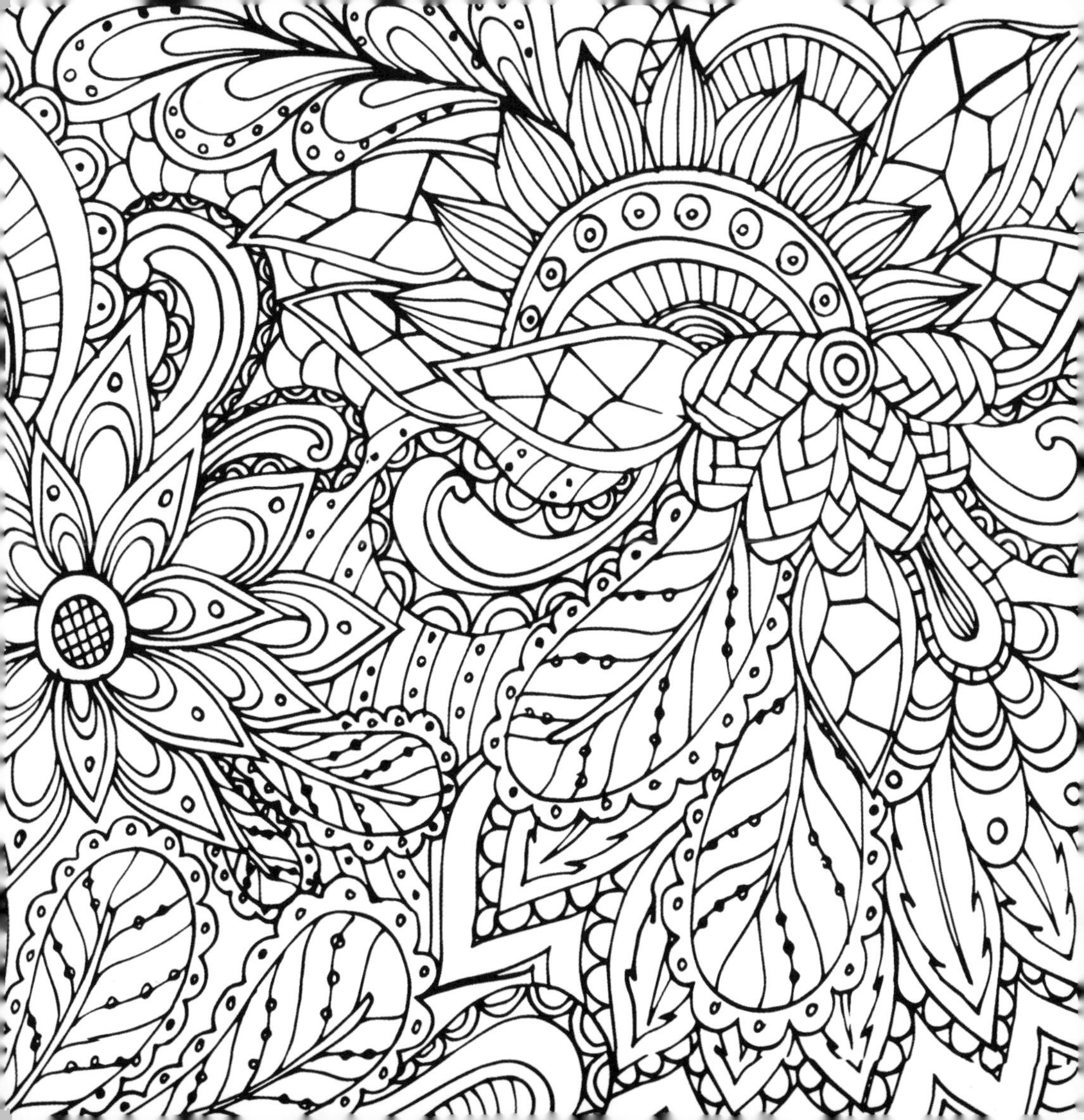

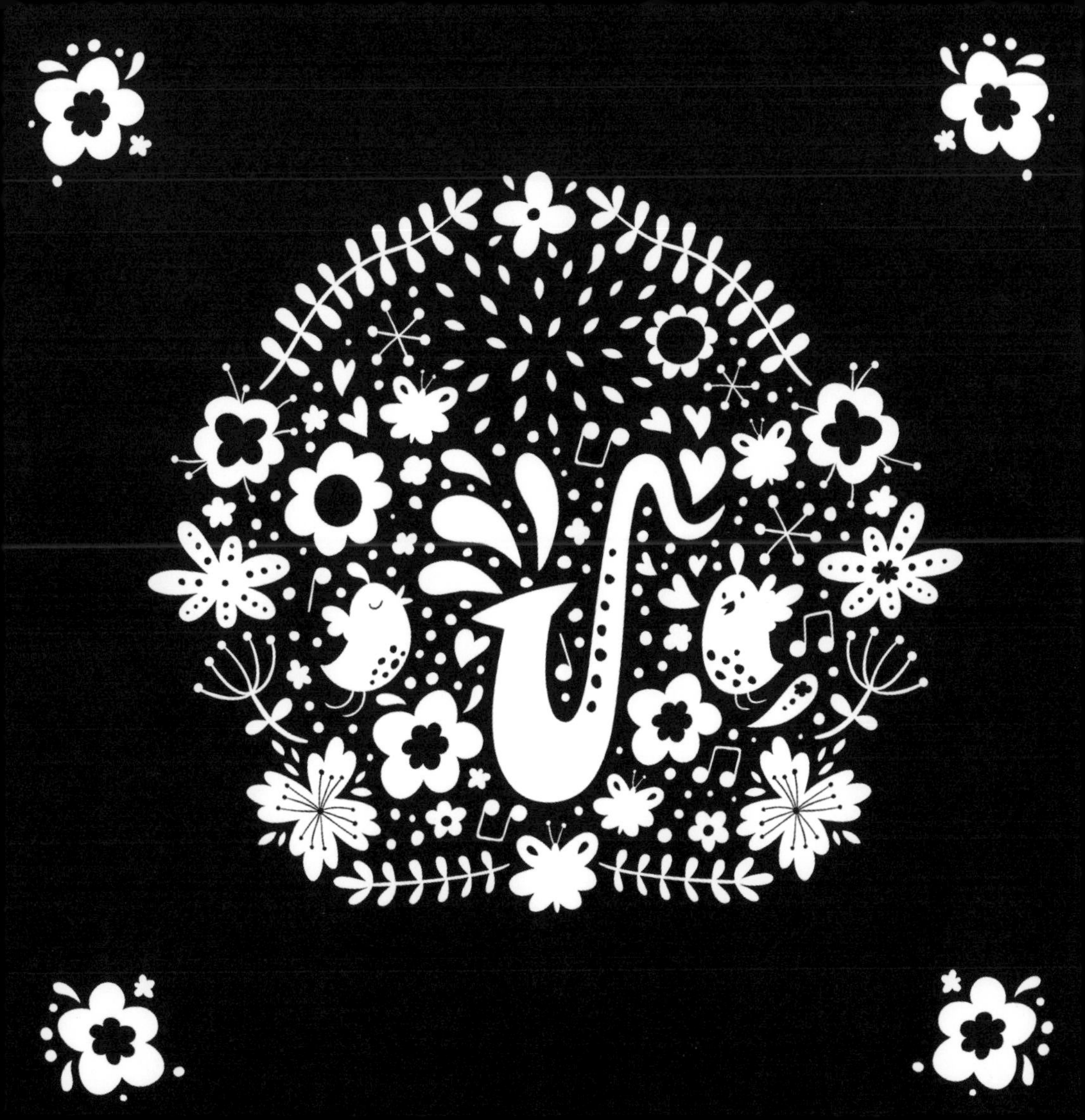

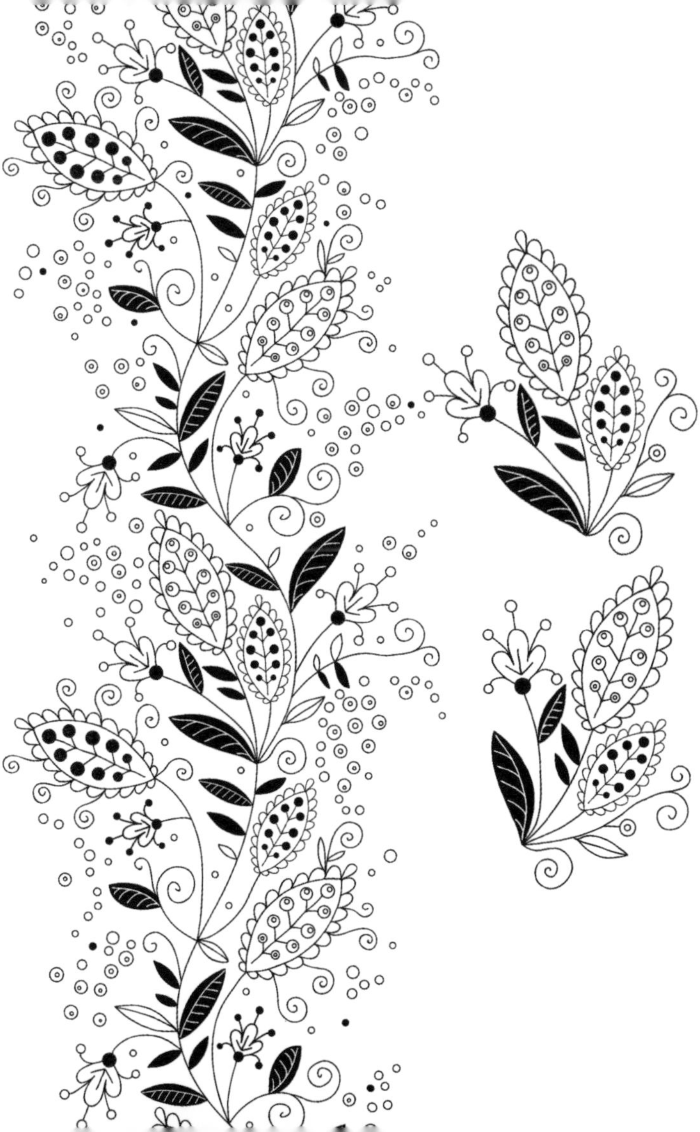

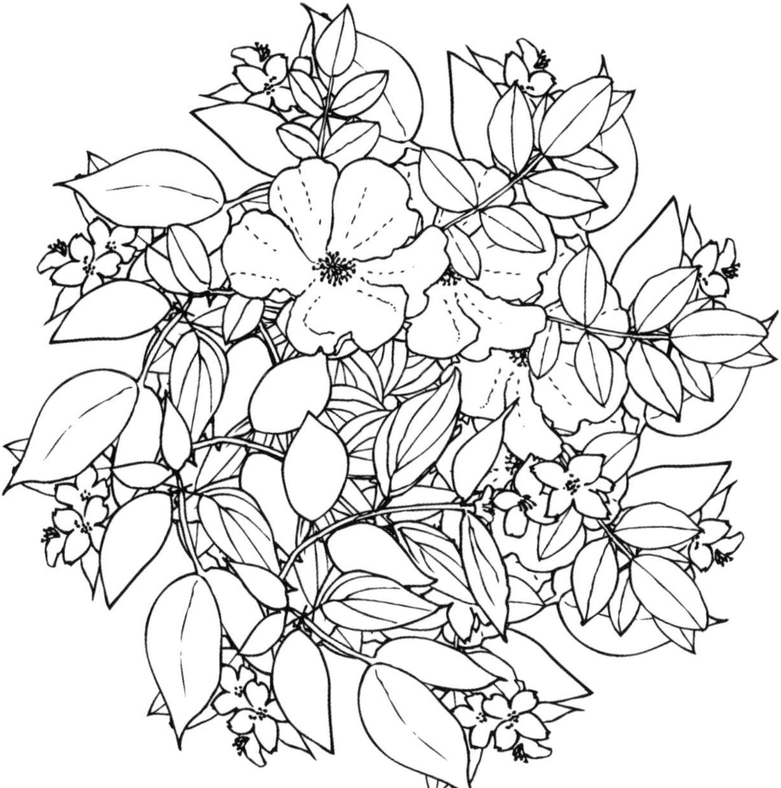

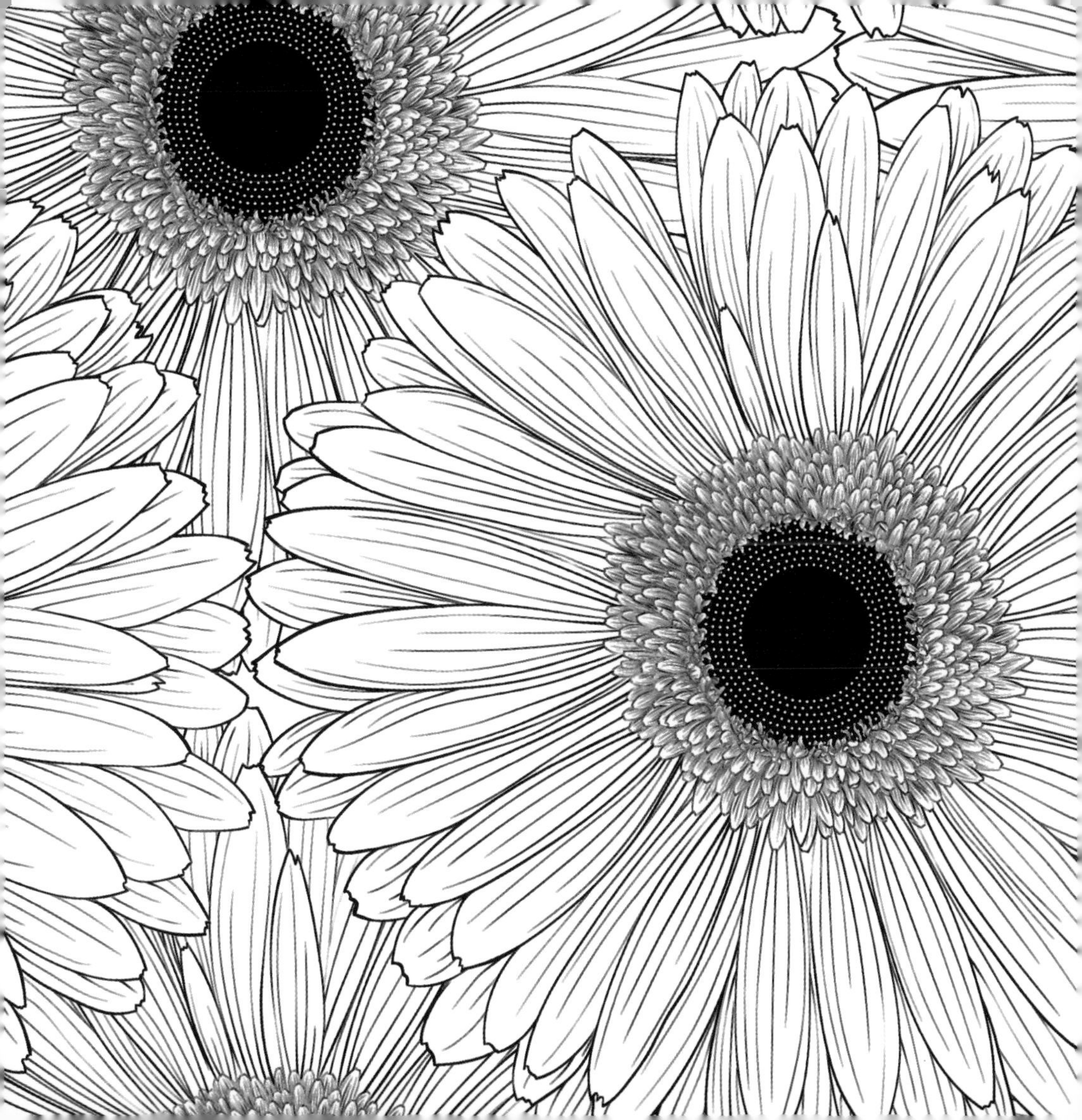

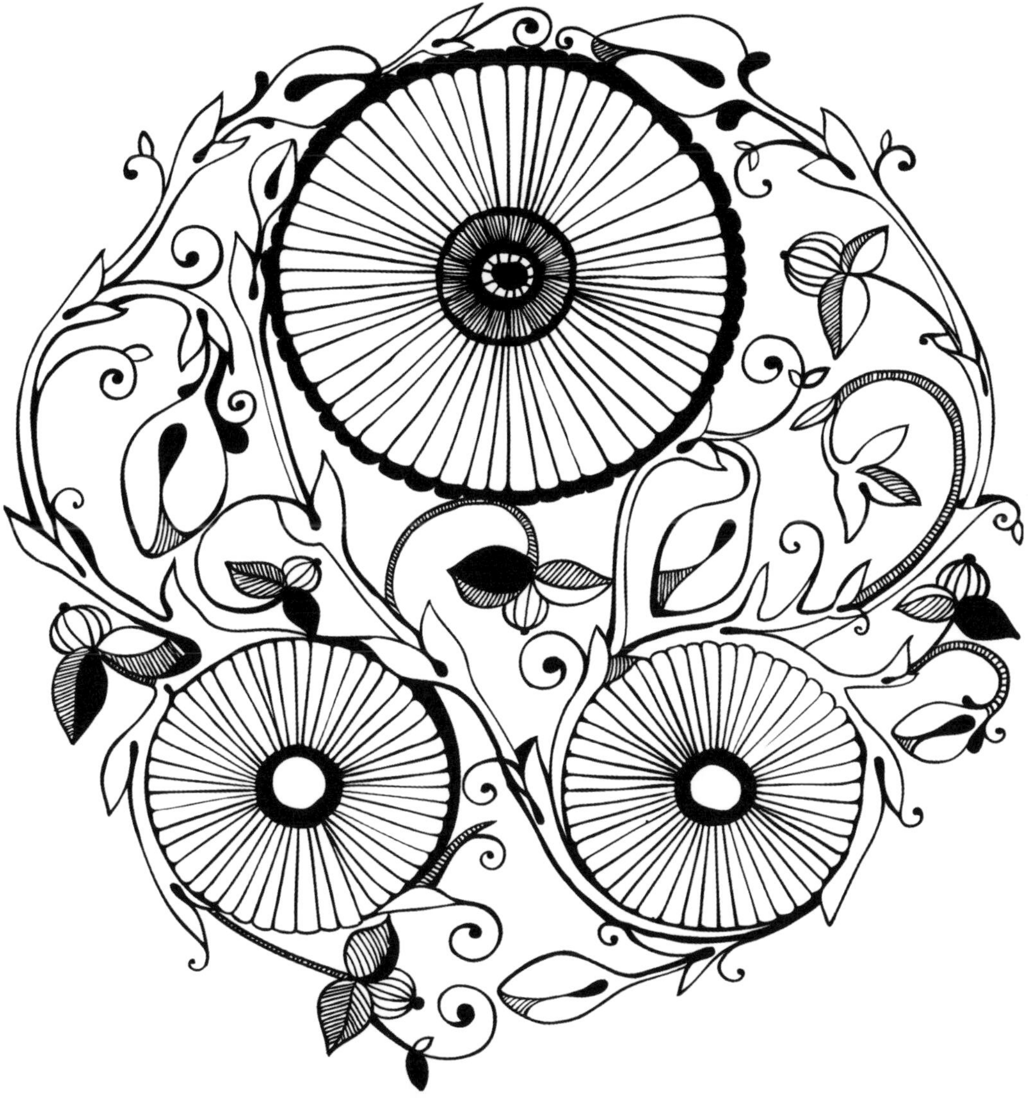

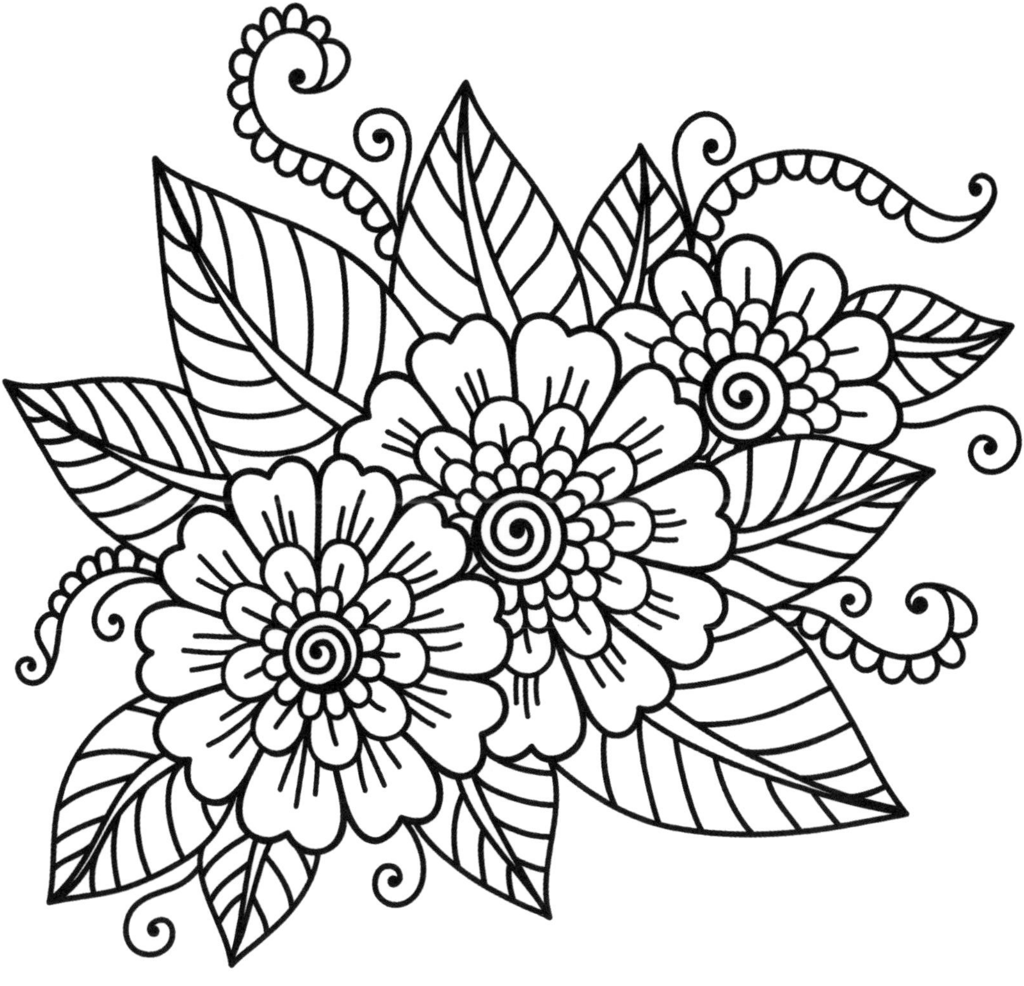

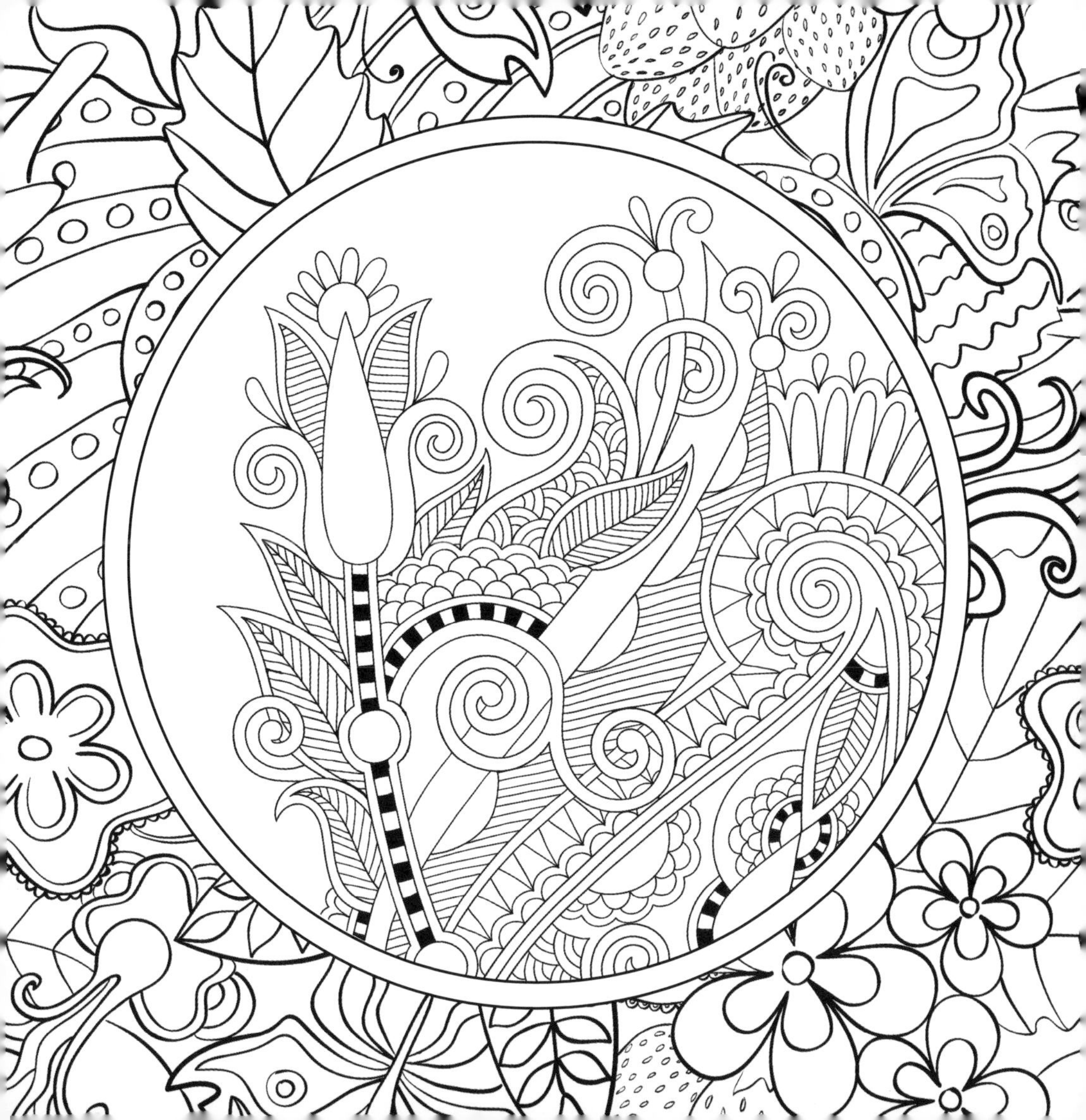

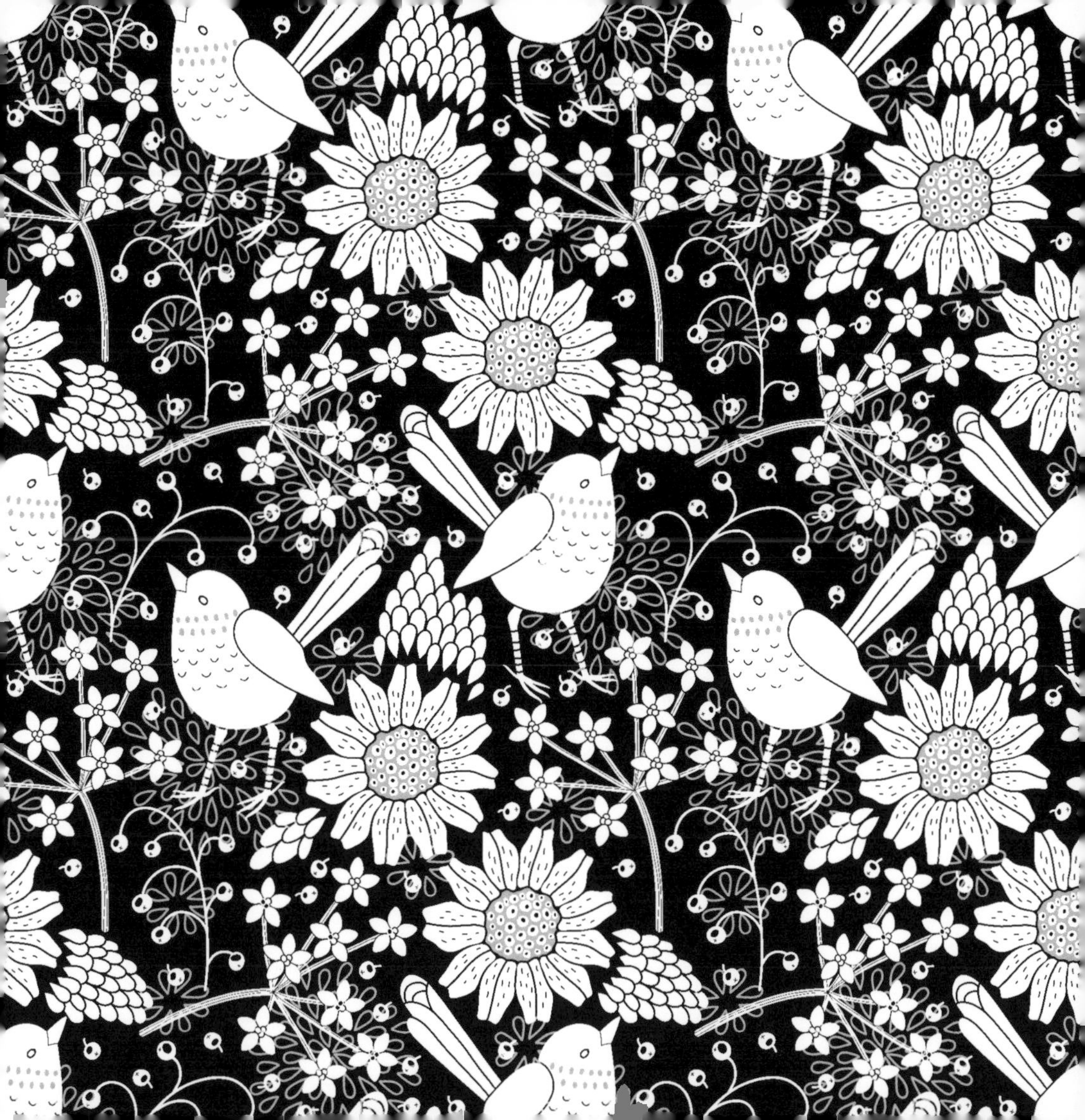